Contents

INTRODUCTION

Your health care provider might recommend that you follow a temporary low residue diet (LRD) if you are recovering from recent bowel surgery (e.g., ileostomy, colostomy, resection), preparing for a colonoscopy, or experiencing heightened symptoms of abdominal pain, cramping, diarrhea, or active digestive flare-ups associated with a gastrointestinal condition, such as Crohn's or diverticular disease.

The term 'residue' refers to any solid contents that end up in the large intestine after digestion. This includes undigested and unabsorbed food (which consists mostly of dietary fibre), bacteria, and gastric secretions.[1] A low residue diet limits dietary fibre to less than 10-15g per day and restricts other foods that could stimulate bowel activity. The goal of a LRD is to decrease the size and frequency of bowel movements in order to reduce painful symptoms. It is similar to a low fibre diet (LFD) except that a LRD also limits some other foods, such as milk, which can increase colonic residue and stool weight.

Low-fiber diet facts

A low-residue diet is a low fiber diet with added restrictions that are designed to reduce the amount of stool in the large intestine.

A low-residue diet is a temporary eating plan with the goal of "resting" the bowel.

Low-residue diets may be prescribed during flares of inflammatory bowel disease (Crohn's disease and ulcerative colitis) before or after bowel surgery, when tumors or narrowing of the intestine exist, or for other conditions.

CHAPTER ONE

LOW RESIDUE DIET

What is a low-fiber (low-residue) diet?

A low-residue diet is a diet that is designed to "rest" the bowel. It is a type of low-fiber diet with added restrictions. A low-residue diet is not a diet plan to follow regularly. It is advised for some people for the short term during a flare of inflammatory bowel disease here is intestinal narrowing, before or after bowel surgery, and other conditions for which it is useful to reduce the amount of stool in the intestines.

The food we eat is digested so that the body can extract the nutrients it needs to function. What's left over is "residue" or undigested food that passes through the colon (large intestine), and is eliminated as stool or feces. A low-residue diet limits fiber and other substances with the goal of reducing stool volume. This results in fewer and smaller bowel movements, potentially relieving symptoms of bowel diseases that can cause inflammation, such as abdominal pain and cramping, bloating, and gas formation.

Who is a low-fiber diet plan for?

In disease and conditions in which the colon has the potential to be inflamed, a low-fiber diet may "rest" the colon. The low-residue diet limits the amount of work the colon has to do in forming feces because most of the content of the diet is absorbed and less waste is required to be eliminated. Since there is a reduced quantity of stool, the time it takes to pass through the length of the colon is increased, resulting in smaller, less frequent bowel movements.

Low-fiber diets are often recommended for patients with a number of different conditions, including the following:

Flares of inflammatory bowel disease, either Crohn's Disease or ulcerative colitis

Vowel tumors

Inflamed bowel due to radiation or chemotherapy treatments

Before or after bowel surgery, or before colonoscopy

Inflammation or narrowing of the bowel

In the past, individuals with diverticulosis or irritable bowel disease syndrome (IBS) might have been prescribed a low-residue diet; however, current recommendations now suggest that a high fiber diet might be of more benefit in these conditions. Special diets may be prescribed during flares of acute bowel inflammation (as with diverticulitis), but a high-fiber diet is generally recommended for people with the diverticular disease as this has been shown to be protective for the development of diverticula.

Any diet like this one that restricts certain foods may also be responsible for the decreased intake of important minerals and vitamins. Calcium, potassium, folic acid, and vitamin C supplements may be required with a low-fiber diet.

Individuals on a low-fiber diet will want to limit their fiber intake to 7-10 grams per day. Read food labels carefully. Most food packaging will list the amount of fiber on their label.

Why eat a low-residue diet?

Usually, physicians can prescribe this diet before or after certain medical procedures like colonoscopy, bowel surgery or in case of tumors or narrowing of the intestine. It may also be suggested to treat symptoms of irritable bowel syndrome, diverticulitis, diarrhea, Crohn's disease, ulcerative colitis. It's important to follow this diet precisely when it's prescribed, as it might cause unpleasant side effects and symptoms if you stick to it incorrectly.

Benefits of low–residue diet

reduce the bowel movements by cutting down on foods that are poorly digested

reduce the amount of stool your body produces

ease abdominal pain, diarrhea, and other symptoms

ease the amount of work your digestive system isn't doing

How It Works

Creating a meal plan that puts as little demand on the digestive tract as possible is the rationale behind a low-residue diet.You'll be able to adapt the diet to your preferred eating schedule, but the content and size of your meals will be different from what you're used to.

The biggest change you'll be making on a low-residue diet is your fiber intake. For an adult eating a regular 2,000 calorie per day diet, the recommendation for daily fiber intake is at least 25 grams (g) per day. On a low-residue diet, you'll be sticking to just 10 to 15 g of fiber per day.

Your doctor and a registered dietician or nutritionist can help you put together meals that work with these dietary restrictions and provide adequate nutrition.

Why do I need a low residue diet?

You may need to follow a low residue diet for one of the following reasons:

•You have a narrowing of the gut (sometimes called a stricture) which means fibre containing foods may not pass through effectively and therefore may cause a blockage.

•You have an inflammation of the lining of the gut wall caused by a disease or by radiotherapy which means that fibre containing foods may aggravate the gut and lead to

diarrhoea.

•As a way to prepare your bowel before certain medical investigations or procedures. In the above instances food is not the cause of the problems but avoiding higher fibre foods may make you feel more comfortable. There is always some trial and error and you may find that you can tolerate small amounts of fibre which will help to make your meals more varied

and interesting.

A low residue diet is usually used as a short term measure only, so keep asking your doctor or dietitian if you still need to follow this diet.

Nutrition and Dietetics

• Vegetables and salad – raw, cooked, tinned or frozen especially the skins and stalks

• Fruit – fresh, frozen, tinned, cooked and dried especially skins

• Beans, lentils and chick peas

• Potatoes with skin on (boiled, baked, roast, chipped)

Practical ways to reduce your fibre intake

• Choose white cereals such as cornflakes or rice based cereals (ideally one fortified in vitamins).

• Choose white varieties of rice and pasta.

• Choose plain white biscuits such as rich tea, custard creams, nice or malted milks.

• Choose white varieties of bread, crumpets and scones.

• Try to avoid the skins of potatoes.

• If you do some home baking try to use white flour.

- All fruit, vegetables and salad items contain fibre especially those which have skins, seeds and pips. Some people find that they can tolerate well boiled or pureed vegetables and fruit but trial cautiously.

- Be careful of added vegetables, fruit, nuts and seeds in ready bought soups, sauces and convenience/readymade meals.

- Include vitamin C containing fruit squash or a small glass of fresh fruit juice (without bits)

to help get a balanced diet while you are restricting a lot of fruit and vegetables.

Foods Allowed on a Low Residue Diet
Grains

Refined or enriched white breads and plain crackers, such as saltines or Melba toast (no seeds)

Cooked cereals, like farina, cream of wheat, and grits

Cold cereals, like puffed rice and corn flakes

White rice, noodles, and refined pasta

Fruits and Vegetables

The skin and seeds of many fruits and vegetables are full of fiber, so you need to peel them and avoid the seeds.

These vegetables are OK:

Well-cooked fresh vegetables or canned vegetables without seeds, like asparagus tips, beets, green beans, carrots, mushrooms, spinach, squash (no seeds), and pumpkin

Cooked potatoes without skin

Tomato sauce (no seeds)

Fruits on the good list include:

Ripe bananas

Soft cantaloupe

Honeydew

Canned or cooked fruits without seeds or skin, like applesauce or canned pears

Avocado

Milk and Dairy

They're OK in moderation. Milk has no fiber, but it may trigger symptoms like diarrhea and cramping if you're lactose intolerant. If you are (meaning you have trouble processing dairy foods), you could take lactase supplements or buy lactose-free products.

Meats

Animal products don't have fiber. You can eat beef, lamb, chicken, fish (no bones), and pork, as long as they're lean, tender, and soft. Eggs are OK, too.

Fats, Sauces, and Condiments

These are all on the diet:

Margarine, butter, and oils

Mayonnaise and ketchup

Sour cream

Smooth sauces and salad dressing

Soy sauce

Clear jelly, honey, and syrup

Sweets and Snacks

You can satisfy your sweet tooth on a low-residue diet. These desserts and snacks are OK to eat in moderation:

Plain cakes and cookies

Gelatin, plain puddings, custard, and sherbet

Ice cream and ice pops

Hard candy

Pretzels (not whole-grain varieties)

Vanilla wafers

Drinks

Safe beverages include:

Decaffeinated coffee, tea, and carbonated beverages (caffeine can upset your stomach)

Milk

Juices made without seeds or pulp, like apple, no-pulp orange, and cranberry

Strained vegetable juices

Foods to Avoid on a Low Residue Diet

Whole grain breads and pastas, corn bread or muffins, products made with whole grain products, or bran

Strong cheeses, yogurt containing fruit skins or seeds

Raw vegetables, except lettuce and other leaves

Tough meat, meat with gristle

Crunchy peanut butter

Millet, buckwheat, flax, oatmeal

Dried beans, peas, and legumes

Dried fruits, berries, other fruits with skin or seeds

Chocolate with Cocoa Powder (white chocolate has no fiber)

Food containing whole coconut

Juices with pulp

Highly spiced food and dressings, pepper, hot sauces

Caffeine

Popcorn

Nuts and Seeds

Limitations of the Low Residue Diet

The LRD may be beneficial for symptom management during heightened or acute episodes of increased abdominal pain, infection, or inflammation. However, be aware that this diet is not recommended for all those suffering with inflammatory bowel disease or other chronic conditions. LRD will not decrease inflammation nor will it improve the underlying cause of your condition. Following a LRD for a prolonged period might lead to nutrient deficiencies and other gastrointestinal symptoms (e.g., constipation).

Drinks and foods that are not on low-fiber diet plan

A low-residue diet encompasses more than eating less fiber. In addition to decreasing the amount of fiber, individuals eating a low-residue diet also should try to restrict foods that increase bowel activity, and make the stools looser. Examples include dairy products and fruit juices such as prune juice that do not have pulp fiber, but do stimulate the bowel.

Low–residue diet menu may look like this.

Breakfast

Decaffeinated coffee (with cream and sugar, if desired)

A cup of pulp-free juice (orange, apple or cranberry juice)

Farina

Scrambled eggs

Waffles, French toast, or pancakes

White-bread toast with margarine and grape jelly (no seeds)

Lunch

Baked chicken, white rice, canned carrots, or green beans

Salad with baked chicken, American cheese, smooth salad dressing, white dinner roll

Baked potato (no skin) with sour cream and butter or margarine

Hamburger with white seedless bun, ketchup, and mayonnaise -- and lettuce if it doesn't make your symptoms worse

Dinner

Tender roast beef, white rice, cooked carrots or spinach, white dinner roll with margarine or butter

Pasta with butter or olive oil, French bread, fruit cocktail

Baked chicken, white rice or baked potato without skin, and cooked green beans

Broiled fish, white rice, and canned green beans

Should You Try a Low-Residue Diet?

Everyone is different. You may be OK with some of the things listed under "foods to avoid," while other items on the "foods to enjoy" list may bother you. So keep a food diary for a few weeks. Track what you eat and how it makes you feel, so you know what works for you.

If you enjoy whole grains, nuts, and raw fruits and vegetables, shifting to a low-residue diet may be hard. But if you prefer white bread and pasta, don't mind canned fruits and vegetables, and are happy to snack on saltines and vanilla wafers, it may come naturally.

Remember, this isn't a healthy way to eat for a long time because it skips many important nutrients.

Ask your doctor if he knows a nutritionist who can help make sure your diet is right for you and let you know if you need to take supplements.

How long will I need to follow a low residue diet for?

The length of time you will need to follow the low residue diet for will depend on the reason you need the diet for. For example, if you are having radiotherapy you will need to continue with the diet for around 2 weeks or until your diarrhoea has resolved before you re-introduce more fibre into your diet. Your nurse, dietitian, doctor or radiographer will give you more detail on how long you need to follow a low residue diet for.

How do I follow this diet if I am vegetarian or have other food intolerances?

If you do not eat meat or fish or have other food intolerances please ask to be referred for individual advice from a dietitian. You should also ask your doctor if you need to be referred to dietitian if you are not eating well or are losing weight before or after starting a low residue diet.

Cost

If you need to take nutritional supplements or probiotics, you may find them to be a high-cost part of your diet. Ask your doctor and health insurance provider if these items can be prescribed for you. If your health insurance won't cover the cost, ask about promotions, coupons, or patient assistance programs for prescriptions.

Side Effects

If you are following a low-residue diet for a longer period of time, you'll want to be aware of the possible signs of a nutritional deficiency.

Fatigue and shortness of breath may indicate iron deficiency anemia. If you aren't getting enough vitamin C, you can develop symptoms of scurvy such as bleeding of your gums, loss of appetite, weight loss, and skin changes. Vitamin B12 deficiency can cause neurological symptoms such as trouble remembering things, numbness and tingling in your limbs, and balance problems.

You may also experience constipation while on a low-fiber diet. Staying hydrated will help you avoid this.3 Following a low-residue diet doesn't mean you can't have any fiber at all. So if constipation is an issue, a fiber supplement may be recommended.

General Health

If a low-residue diet isn't enough to treat your symptoms, your doctor might suggest you try a probiotic and/or you may be prescribed a course of antibiotics.

Probiotic supplements don't treat digestive disorders, but an imbalance of gut bacteria may cause or worsen symptoms.

Antibiotics may be necessary if you have small intestinal bacterial overgrowth (SIBO) or another type of bacterial infection, or if you are undergoing surgery.

Low-Residue vs. Other Diets

A low-residue diet has very specific requirements, but it is similar to other types of diets commonly used to treat bowel disorders.

Low-Fiber Diet

A low-fiber diet is part of a low-residue diet. The main difference between the two diets is that if you're following a low-residue diet, you'll have added restrictions.

One of the biggest differences between a low-fiber diet and low-residue diet is how much dairy is allowed.

Dairy is allowed on a low-fiber diet to the degree you personally tolerate it. But if you're on a low-residue diet, you can only have 2 cups of dairy products a day.

Your daily fiber allowance on both a low-fiber and low-residue diet will be about 10 to 15 grams per day.

Low-FODMAP Diet

Fermentable oligosaccharides, disaccharides, monosaccharides, and polyols (FODMAPs) are found in many of the foods we eat. Some people find FODMAP-containing foods cause or worsen symptoms of digestive disorders like irritable bowel syndrome (IBS), such as bloating, abdominal pain, and diarrhea.

A low-FODMAP diet is similar to a low-residue diet, but not entirely. Many of the foods you can eat on a low-FODMAP diet are not permitted on a low-residue diet, including nuts and seeds, broccoli, brown rice, and oats. Foods with a lot of fiber such as legumes and beans, apples, and okra are also considered high-FODMAP foods.

Dairy typically isn't allowed on a low-FODMAP diet, but on a low-residue diet, you can have less than 2 cups of dairy each day if you tolerate it.

BRAT Diet

The BRAT Diet is commonly used to treat temporary digestive upsets like a viral stomach flu or food poisoning. BRAT is an acronym for bananas, plain white rice, applesauce, and toast made with refined white bread—foods that are easy to digest if you are experiencing symptoms like nausea and diarrhea.

While the BRAT Diet works well in the short-term, you shouldn't stay on the diet for a long time unless your doctor is supervising you. It's difficult to get all the energy and nutrition your body needs if you're only eating small amounts of a limited group of foods.

The low residue diet can help with bowel disease

The low residue diet is a short-term plan to give your digestive system a break from breaking down hard-to-digest foods, says Lori Welstead, a dietician who works in gastroenterology at the University of Chicago Medical Center. "It is not recommended to be lifelong in most cases."

The dietician recommends following the low fiber diet only as long as you are having symptoms like diarrhea. Once your symptoms have improved, you can start slowly reintroducing fiber into your diet.

However, research is divided on whether a low fiber diet is truly helpful for all types of inflammatory conditions.

For example, a study published in Clinical Gastroenterology and Hepatology in 2016, found that among patients in remission, avoiding fiber was linked to an increased risk of flare-ups for people with Crohn's disease.

In addition, a review of 23 studies, published in Inflammatory Bowel Disease in 2014, found that overall, there is no evidence to support restricting fiber when treating IBD. And other studies have found similar results, suggesting that diets that cut out specific foods like gluten or legumes worked better for IBD than a low-fiber diet.

The low-residue diet and GI procedure prep

If you've ever had a colonoscopy and dreaded the preparation, the low-residue diet might help abate some discomfort. Traditionally, patients who are going in for a GI procedure are told that they must stick to a clear liquid diet the day before.

But a number of studies have shown that a low-residue diet may be just as effective at colon preparation while vastly improving patient satisfaction. If you're going in for a GI procedure, ask your doctor if you can swap water and broth for more filling, low-residue options.

Low-fiber diets aren't meant to last

The low residue diet is not the only diet out there that can help with gastrointestinal symptoms. The following other diets can be used to help control diarrhea in the short term, but none of them are long-term solutions.

The BRAT (bananas, rice, applesauce, and toast) diet is meant to help your body recover from symptoms like vomiting and diarrhea, usually from a stomach bug.

Because it's so restrictive, you should only follow it for one to two days.

The low FODMAP (Fermentable, Oligo, Disaccharides and Polyols) diet limits certain types of carbohydrates than can cause gastro symptoms like gas, bloating, and diarrhea, Welstead says. However, this diet is used more as a diagnostic tool than a long-term meal plan. "The low FODMAP diet is only recommended for a short period to determine what foods are trigger foods," Welstead says.

Welstead warns that sticking to a restrictive diet like the low residue diet can cause deficiencies in vitamin or protein levels. "For most patients, they are able to transition to a normal diet over time," Welstead adds.

That's why you should speak with a registered dietitian before starting any of these diets, including the low residue diet.

Considerations

Making changes to your diet requires you to think about more than what you can and can't eat. Here are a few other considerations to keep in mind.

Sustainability and Practicality

Many foods approved on a low-residue diet are plentiful at markets and grocery stores. Stock up on non-perishable items like boxed pasta and canned goods to have on hand if symptoms pop up suddenly.

If you are unable to prepare fruits and vegetables according to the diet (peeling and cooking, for instance) many varieties can be bought pre-cut, pre-cooked, or already peeled. You can also get pureed versions of many fruits and vegetables, which can be eaten as-is or added to smoothies, sauces, etc.

Flexibility

Whenever you're planning to change up how you eat, you'll need to take the reality of your day-to-day schedule into account. Some diets can be challenging if you can't plan ahead, but many approved foods on a low-residue diet are readily available at the grocery store or can be easily packed as a snack.

Even dining out on a low-residue diet is possible as long as you ask about how food is prepared, what ingredients are included in the dish, and know when to ask for modifications (such as swapping white bread instead of wheat).

Dietary Restrictions

If you follow a special diet for another reason, such as a food allergy, you'll need to carefully consider any diet that further restricts what you're allowed to eat.

For example, if you're on a gluten-free diet, you probably already avoid many of the whole grains and carbohydrates that aren't on the approved low-residue food list.

However, you'll need to pay careful attention to the ingredients commonly used to make gluten-free bread, pasta, and cereals, including nuts, seeds, and brown rice.

If you follow a vegan or vegetarian diet, low-residue animal products, such as meat, eggs, and dairy, would be excluded. The typical alternative sources of protein for plant-based diets, like beans and legumes, are not approved for a low-residue diet.

Handy hints

Eat small meals at regular intervals (every three to four hours)

Chew food slowly and thoroughly

Avoid food that is too hot or too cold

When introducing new foods, introduce only one at a time. This will help you to rule out foods that aggravate your symptoms

Avoid large quantities of caffeine or alcohol as these may worsen your symptoms

Avoid rich sauces and spicy foods if they worsen your symptoms

It is important to maintain a good variety of foods, especially if you follow these guidelines for more than a few weeks

Large volumes of milk may not be well tolerated. If so, just use small quantities (in tea and coffee, for example)

Avoid fizzy drinks if they worsen your symptoms

Be cautious with ready meals and pre-prepared foods as they may contain some of the ingredients known to aggravate your symptoms

If eating is difficult, speak to your dietitian about ways to increase your calorie and protein intake to ensure adequate nutrition. Nutritional supplements may be considered. Your dietitian may recommend a multi-vitamin and mineral supplement.

FAQs

What is the difference between low residue diet and low fiber diet?

Both of them are quite resemblant, except for the fact that a low-residue diet demands limiting the consumption of dairy products, so you wouldn't run the risk of increasing colonic residue and stool weight. The bottom line is that you'll give your gastrointestinal tract a much needed break.

Clear liquid diet for diverticulitis

Diverticulitis is a digestive tract disorder that causes inflamed pouches (also called diverticula) in the lining of your intestine. More than 75 percent of diverticulitis cases are uncomplicated, leaving about 25 percent to develop complications. These may include nausea, fever, severe abdominal pain, bloody bowel movements, abscess, etc., but a proper diet can alleviate the symptoms of the disease. There are no specific foods that everyone with diverticulitis has to keep away from. However, as a rule, doctors prescribe low fiber diets during an acute attack of diverticulitis. Moreover, they might even recommend sticking to a clear liquid diet that excludes solid foods altogether.

Following this diet for a few days will help your digestive system to heal, rest and recover. Some studies have linked high-fiber diets to a reduced risk of diverticulitis. Other studies have examined possible benefits of dietary or supplemental fiber for diverticular disease, but they are still unsure whether fiber can help treat it.

One study shows that a low-fiber diet can increase the risk of diverticulitis, however, other researches show that there is no link between low-residue and this disease. Diverticulitis and low-fiber diet need to be studied further, as the results of the researches are quite mixed and inconclusive.

How long to stay on the low-residue diet after diverticulitis?

There is no single right answer to this question, as everything depends on your health condition. Most people stick to this eating pattern until all symptoms subside (diarrhea, cramps). Make sure to increase your fiber intake slowly to avoid stomach aches. The safest option is to introduce one new fiber food a day. Drink plenty of water to ease the transition period.

Consider choosing a workout program to follow that will correspond your health, needs and interests. Physical activity does not only strengthen your body, but also will help you get rid of excess weight, build your muscles and improve your mood.

CHAPTER TWO

LOW RESIDUE DIET RECIPE

Rosemary Roasted Turkey

Ingredients

¾ cup olive oil

3 tablespoons minced garlic

2 tablespoons chopped fresh rosemary

1 tablespoon chopped fresh basil

1 tablespoon Italian seasoning

1 teaspoon ground black pepper

salt to taste

1 (12 pound) whole turkey

Directions

Step 1

Preheat oven to 325 degrees F (165 degrees C).

Step 2

In a small bowl, mix the olive oil, garlic, rosemary, basil, Italian seasoning, black pepper and salt. Set aside.

Step 3

Wash the turkey inside and out; pat dry. Remove any large fat deposits. Loosen the skin from the breast. This is done by slowly working your fingers between the breast and the skin. Work it loose to the end of the drumstick, being careful not to tear the skin.

Step 4

Using your hand, spread a generous amount of the rosemary mixture under the breast skin and down the thigh and leg. Rub the remainder of the rosemary mixture over the outside of the breast. Use toothpicks to seal skin over any exposed breast meat.

Step 5

Place the turkey on a rack in a roasting pan. Add about 1/4 inch of water to the bottom of the pan. Roast in the preheated oven 3 to 4 hours, or until the internal temperature of the bird reaches 180 degrees F (80 degrees C).

Guacamole

Ingredients

3 avocados - peeled, pitted, and mashed

1 lime, juiced

1 teaspoon salt

½ cup diced onion

3 tablespoons chopped fresh cilantro

2 roma (plum) tomatoes, diced

1 teaspoon minced garlic

1 pinch ground cayenne pepper (optional)

Directions

Step 1

In a medium bowl, mash together the avocados, lime juice, and salt. Mix in onion, cilantro, tomatoes, and garlic. Stir in cayenne pepper. Refrigerate 1 hour for best flavor, or serve immediately.

Spiced Sweet Roasted Red Pepper Hummus

Ingredients

1 (15 ounce) can garbanzo beans, drained

1 (4 ounce) jar roasted red peppers

3 tablespoons lemon juice

1 ½ tablespoons tahini

1 clove garlic, minced

½ teaspoon ground cumin

½ teaspoon cayenne pepper

¼ teaspoon salt

1 tablespoon chopped fresh parsley

Directions

Step 1

In an electric blender or food processor, puree the chickpeas, red peppers, lemon juice, tahini, garlic, cumin, cayenne, and salt. Process, using long pulses, until the mixture is fairly smooth, and slightly fluffy. Make sure to scrape the mixture off the sides of the food processor or blender in between pulses. Transfer to a serving bowl and refrigerate for at least 1 hour. (The hummus can be made up to 3 days ahead and refrigerated. Return to room temperature before serving.)

Step 2

Sprinkle the hummus with the chopped parsley before serving.

Foolproof Rib Roast

Ingredients

1 (5 pound) standing beef rib roast

2 teaspoons salt

1 teaspoon ground black pepper

1 teaspoon garlic powder

Directions

Step 1

Allow roast to stand at room temperature for at least 1 hour.

Step 2

Preheat the oven to 375 degrees F (190 degrees C). Combine the salt, pepper and garlic powder in a small cup. Place the roast on a rack in a roasting pan so that the fatty side is up and the rib side is on the bottom. Rub the seasoning onto the roast.

Step 3

Roast for 1 hour in the preheated oven. Turn the oven off and leave the roast inside. Do not open the door. Leave it in there for 3 hours. 30 to 40 minutes before serving, turn the oven back on at 375 degrees F (190 degrees C) to reheat the roast. The internal temperature should be at least 145 degrees F (62 degrees C). Remove from the oven and let rest for 10 minutes before carving into servings.

Spinach and Feta Pita Bake

Ingredients

1 (6 ounce) tub sun-dried tomato pesto

6 (6 inch) whole wheat pita breads

2 roma (plum) tomatoes, chopped

1 bunch spinach, rinsed and chopped

4 fresh mushrooms, sliced

½ cup crumbled feta cheese

2 tablespoons grated Parmesan cheese

3 tablespoons olive oil

ground black pepper to taste

Directions

Step 1

Preheat the oven to 350 degrees F (175 degrees C).

Step 2

Spread tomato pesto onto one side of each pita bread and place them pesto-side up on a baking sheet. Top pitas with tomatoes, spinach, mushrooms, feta cheese, and Parmesan cheese; drizzle with olive oil and season with pepper.

Step 3

Bake in the preheated oven until pita breads are crisp, about 12 minutes. Cut pitas into quarters.

Baked Chicken Wings

Ingredients

3 tablespoons olive oil

3 cloves garlic, pressed

2 teaspoons chili powder

1 teaspoon garlic powder

1 pinch salt and ground black pepper to taste

10 eaches chicken wings

Directions

Step 1

Preheat the oven to 375 degrees F (190 degrees C).

Step 2

Combine the olive oil, garlic, chili powder, garlic powder, salt, and pepper in a large, resealable bag; seal and shake to combine. Add the chicken wings; reseal and shake to coat. Arrange the chicken wings on a baking sheet.

Step 3

Cook the wings in the preheated oven 1 hour, or until crisp and cooked through.

Juicy Roasted Chicken
Ingredients

1 (3 pound) whole chicken, giblets removed

1 teaspoon salt and black pepper to taste

1 tablespoon onion powder, or to taste

½ cup margarine, divided

1 stalk celery, leaves removed

Directions

Step 1

Preheat oven to 350 degrees F (175 degrees C).

Step 2

Place chicken in a roasting pan, and season generously inside and out with salt and pepper. Sprinkle inside and out with onion powder. Place 3 tablespoons margarine in the chicken cavity. Arrange dollops of the remaining margarine around the chicken's exterior. Cut the celery into 3 or 4 pieces, and place in the chicken cavity.

Step 3

Bake uncovered 1 hour and 15 minutes in the preheated oven, to a minimum internal temperature of 180 degrees F (82 degrees C). Remove from heat, and baste with melted margarine and drippings. Cover with aluminum foil, and allow to rest about 30 minutes before serving.

Roast Sticky Chicken-Rotisserie Style

Ingredients

4 teaspoons salt

2 teaspoons paprika

1 teaspoon onion powder

1 teaspoon dried thyme

1 teaspoon white pepper

½ teaspoon cayenne pepper

½ teaspoon black pepper

½ teaspoon garlic powder

2 onions, quartered

2 (4 pound) whole chickens

Directions

Step 1

In a small bowl, mix together salt, paprika, onion powder, thyme, white pepper, black pepper, cayenne pepper, and garlic powder. Remove and discard giblets from chicken. Rinse chicken cavity, and pat dry with paper towel. Rub each chicken inside and out with spice mixture. Place 1 onion into the cavity of each chicken. Place chickens in a resealable bag or double wrap with plastic wrap. Refrigerate overnight, or at least 4 to 6 hours.

Step 2

Preheat oven to 250 degrees F (120 degrees C).

Step 3

Place chickens in a roasting pan. Bake uncovered for 5 hours, to a minimum internal temperature of 180 degrees F (85 degrees C). Let the chickens stand for 10 minutes before carving.

Whole Chicken Slow Cooker Recipe

Ingredients

4 teaspoons salt, or to taste

2 teaspoons paprika

1 teaspoon cayenne pepper

1 teaspoon onion powder

1 teaspoon ground thyme

1 teaspoon ground white pepper

½ teaspoon garlic powder

½ teaspoon ground black pepper

1 whole whole chicken

Directions

Step 1

Mix salt, paprika, cayenne pepper, onion powder, thyme, white pepper, garlic powder, and black pepper together in a small bowl.

Step 2

Rub seasoning mixture over the entire chicken to evenly season. Put rubbed chicken into a large resealable plastic bag; refrigerate 8 hours to overnight.

Step 3

Remove chicken from bag and cook in slow cooker on Low until no longer pink at the bone and the juices run clear, 4 to 8 hours. An instant-read thermometer inserted into the thickest part of the thigh, near the bone should read 165 degrees F (74 degrees C).

Grilled Asparagus

Ingredients

1 pound fresh asparagus spears, trimmed

1 tablespoon olive oil

salt and pepper to taste

Directions

Step 1

Preheat grill for high heat.

Step 2

Lightly coat the asparagus spears with olive oil. Season with salt and pepper to taste.

Step 3

Grill over high heat for 2 to 3 minutes, or to desired tenderness.

Garlic Prime Rib
Ingredients

1 (10 pound) prime rib roast

10 cloves garlic, minced

2 tablespoons olive oil

2 teaspoons salt

2 teaspoons ground black pepper

2 teaspoons dried thyme

Directions

Step 1

Place the roast in a roasting pan with the fatty side up. In a small bowl, mix together the garlic, olive oil, salt, pepper and thyme. Spread the mixture over the fatty layer of the roast, and let the roast sit out until it is at room temperature, no longer than 1 hour.

Step 2

Preheat the oven to 500 degrees F (260 degrees C).

Step 3

Bake the roast for 20 minutes in the preheated oven, then reduce the temperature to 325 degrees F (165 degrees C), and continue roasting for an additional 60 to 75 minutes. The internal temperature of the roast should be at 135 degrees F (57 degrees C) for medium rare.

Step 4

Allow the roast to rest for 10 or 15 minutes before carving so the meat can retain its juices.

Simple Roasted Butternut Squash

Ingredients

1 butternut squash - peeled, seeded, and cut into 1-inch cubes

2 tablespoons olive oil

2 cloves garlic, minced

salt and ground black pepper to taste

Directions

Step 1

Preheat oven to 400 degrees F (200 degrees C).

Step 2

Toss butternut squash with olive oil and garlic in a large bowl. Season with salt and black pepper. Arrange coated squash on a baking sheet.

Step 3

Roast in the preheated oven until squash is tender and lightly browned, 25 to 30 minutes.

Marinated Grilled Shrimp

Ingredients

3 cloves garlic, minced

⅓ cup olive oil

¼ cup tomato sauce

2 tablespoons red wine vinegar

2 tablespoons chopped fresh basil

½ teaspoon salt

¼ teaspoon cayenne pepper

2 pounds fresh shrimp, peeled and deveined

6 eaches skewers

Directions

Step 1

In a large bowl, stir together the garlic, olive oil, tomato sauce, and red wine vinegar. Season with basil, salt, and cayenne pepper. Add shrimp to the bowl, and stir until evenly coated. Cover, and refrigerate for 30 minutes to 1 hour, stirring once or twice.

Step 2

Preheat grill for medium heat. Thread shrimp onto skewers, piercing once near the tail and once near the head. Discard marinade.

Step 3

Lightly oil grill grate. Cook shrimp on preheated grill for 2 to 3 minutes per side, or until opaque.

Ken's Perfect Hard Boiled Egg (And I Mean Perfect)

Ingredients

1 tablespoon salt

¼ cup distilled white vinegar

6 cups water

8 eggs

Directions

Step 1

Combine the salt, vinegar, and water in a large pot, and bring to a boil over high heat. Add the eggs one at a time, being careful not to crack them. Reduce the heat to a gentle boil, and cook for 14 minutes.

Step 2

Once the eggs have cooked, remove them from the hot water, and place into a container of ice water or cold, running water. Cool completely, about 15 minutes. Store in the refrigerator up to 1 week.

Pico de Gallo

Ingredients

6 roma (plum) tomatoes, diced

½ red onion, minced

3 tablespoons chopped fresh cilantro

½ jalapeno pepper, seeded and minced

½ lime, juiced

1 clove garlic, minced

1 pinch garlic powder

1 pinch ground cumin, or to taste

1 pinch salt and ground black pepper to taste

Directions

Step 1

Stir the tomatoes, onion, cilantro, jalapeno pepper, lime juice, garlic, garlic powder, cumin, salt, and pepper together in a bowl. Refrigerate at least 3 hours before serving.

Simple Grilled Lamb Chops

Ingredients

¼ cup distilled white vinegar

2 teaspoons salt

½ teaspoon black pepper

1 tablespoon minced garlic

1 onion, thinly sliced

2 tablespoons olive oil

2 pounds lamb chops

Directions

Step 1

Mix together the vinegar, salt, pepper, garlic, onion, and olive oil in a large resealable bag until the salt has dissolved. Add lamb, toss until coated, and marinate in refrigerator for 2 hours.

Step 2

Preheat an outdoor grill for medium-high heat.

Step 3

Remove lamb from the marinade and leave any onions on that stick to the meat. Discard any remaining marinade. Wrap the exposed ends of the bones with aluminum foil to keep them from burning. Grill to desired doneness, about 3 minutes per side for medium. The chops may also be broiled in the oven about 5 minutes per side for medium.

Fresh Tomato Salsa

Ingredients

3 tomatoes, chopped

½ cup finely diced onion

5 eaches serrano chiles, finely chopped

½ cup chopped fresh cilantro

1 teaspoon salt

2 teaspoons lime juice

Directions

Step 1

In a medium bowl, stir together tomatoes, onion, chili peppers, cilantro, salt, and lime juice. Chill for one hour in the refrigerator before serving.

Fruity Fun Skewers

Ingredients

5 large strawberries, halved

¼ cantaloupe, cut into balls or cubes

2 eaches bananas, peeled and cut into chunks

1 apple, cut into chunks

20 eaches skewers

Directions

Step 1

Thread the strawberries, cantaloupe, banana and apple pieces alternately onto skewers, placing at least 2 pieces of fruit on each skewer. Arrange the fruit skewers decoratively on a serving platter.

Roasted Brussels Sprouts

Ingredients

1 ½ pounds Brussels sprouts, ends trimmed and yellow leaves removed

3 tablespoons olive oil

1 teaspoon kosher salt

½ teaspoon freshly ground black pepper

Directions

Step 1

Preheat oven to 400 degrees F (205 degrees C).

Step 2

Place trimmed Brussels sprouts, olive oil, kosher salt, and pepper in a large resealable plastic bag. Seal tightly, and shake to coat. Pour onto a baking sheet, and place on center oven rack.

Step 3

Roast in the preheated oven for 30 to 45 minutes, shaking pan every 5 to 7 minutes for even browning. Reduce heat when necessary to prevent burning. Brussels sprouts should be darkest brown, almost black, when done. Adjust seasoning with kosher salt, if necessary. Serve immediately.

Roast Chicken with Rosemary
Ingredients

1 (3 pound) whole chicken, rinsed

salt and pepper to taste

1 small onion, quartered

¼ cup chopped fresh rosemary

Directions

Step 1

Preheat oven to 350 degrees F (175 degrees C).

Step 2

Season chicken with salt and pepper to taste. Stuff with the onion and rosemary. Place chicken in a 9x13 inch baking dish or roasting dish.

Step 3

Roast in the preheated oven for 2 to 2 1/2 hours, or until chicken is cooked through and juices run clear. Cooking time will vary a bit depending on the size of the bird.

CHAPTER THREE

CONCLUSION

Compared to your typical diet, you may feel your food choices on a low-residue diet are limited and bland. That's true. And while perhaps disappointing, it's part of why the diet works to help you manage gastrointestinal symptoms. Work with your doctor and a dietitian to create a meal plan that addresses your symptoms, preferences, and nutritional needs. The longer you are on a low-residue diet, the harder it becomes to stay properly nourished.

Printed in Great Britain
by Amazon

23622228R00030